BIRMINGHAM FROM THE AIR

BIRMINGHAM FROM THE AIR

WEBBAVIATION.CO.UK

breedon books
PUBLISHING

First published in Great Britain in 2009 by
The Breedon Books Publishing Company Limited
Breedon House, 3 The Parker Centre,
Derby, DE21 4SZ.

© Webb Aviation, 2009

ISBN 978-1-85983-688-0

Printed and bound in Gutenberg Press Ltd, Malta.

Acknowledgments

There are a number of people who have helped in the making of this book, and I would like to express particular thanks to John Seville, the UK's best 'photobatic' pilot, and of course Birmingham Air Traffic Control who are always very helpful and are brilliant at keeping small planes flying circles away from big planes flying straight lines. I would also like to thank fellow aerial photographers William Cross and Catherine Wheildon, my brother Nicholas and sister-in-law Melanie for their local knowledge and my long-suffering partner Birgit Engstfeld for putting up with me!

Contents

Introduction

Birmingham is a city packed with stories to tell, with architecture ranging from the mediaeval period to the 21st century and with 2,000 years of recorded history covering invasions by Romans, Saxons and Normans. Each have left their legacy, from the Roman Fort to the Saxon street and place names which are still in use to this day.

Birmingham was the birth place of the Industrial Revolution with the Soho Manufactory leading the way for mass production and Cadbury's at Bournville showing how world-beating production could be combined with a pleasant environment. I have included all the most important subjects you would expect, such as the Council House, Beetham Tower, BT Tower, but also some of the less well-known gems, such as Selly Manor and the Saracens Head. I have also included a few surprises, such as the St Patrick's Day Parade and even the Bronze Bull in the Bullring.

For the photography I have used the very latest Canon 1DS mkIII camera, which I have mounted on a gyro stabilizer. The Gyro contains two titanium discs which spin at 20,000 rpm, thus holding the unit steady, even when the aircraft is moving. When coupled with image-stabilized super-long-lenses, this allows close-up aerial photography with a resolution the city has not seen before.

Architecture

Above, opposite and previous page: The Council House.
Designed by Yeoville Thomason, the Council House took five years to build at a cost of £163,000 and was opened in 1879. The extension (above) was added in 1885. The Grade II listed building is home to Birmingham City Council, and the clock is known as 'Big Brum'. In front of the Council House in the middle of Victoria Square is a large fountain with a 1.75-tonne statue called The River by Dhruva Mistry, which is known locally as the 'Floozie in the Jacuzzi'!

Above: The Central Methodist Hall.
Constructed between 1903 and 1904, the Central Methodist Hall was designed by E. and J. A. Harper and received a Grade II listing in 1970. The building stands in the Steelhouse conservation area and currently contains a central hall, surrounded by a balcony, with its original organ pipes and a grand staircase. There are, however, plans to convert the building into flats, which would see the loss of some of the original interior.

Opposite: West Midlands Fire Service headquarters at Lancaster Circus.
Constructed in 1934 and opened in 1935, the building has been recently replaced by a new headquarters and faces an uncertain future.

Left: The Beetham Tower on Holloway Circus.

Designed by Ian Simpson Architects, the Beetham Tower is 130m high and contains 40 stories. Originally it was intended to be 44 stories, but the design had to be shortened a little following concerns about its height. The lower 18 floors of the building are occupied by the 220-bedroom Radisson Hotel, with the remainder being 156 luxury residential apartments. The design is noted for squeezing a landmark building on a tiny plot of land less than one-third of an acre in size and for having won a RIBA Housing Design Award.

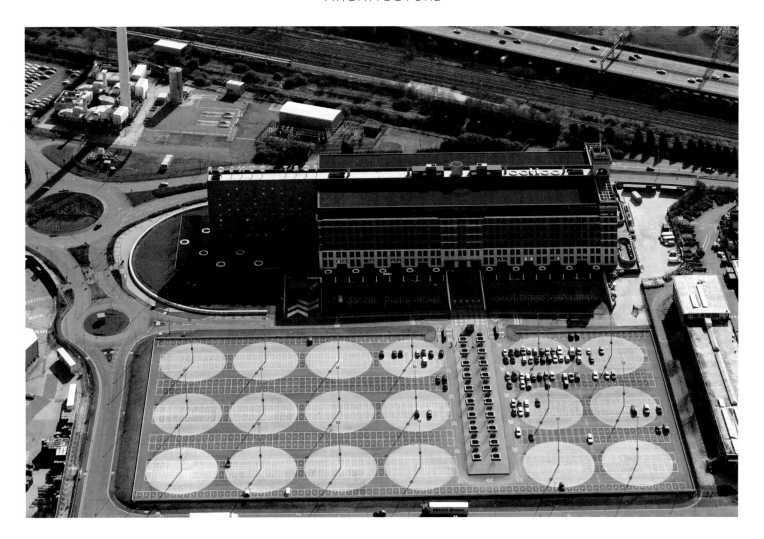

Above: Fort Dunlop.

Once the largest factory in the world with space for more than 3,000 workers, the iconic building was originally designed by Sidney Stott and W.W. Gibbings in the 1920s. When tyre manufacture ceased, the building lay derelict for 20 years but has recently been redeveloped by Urban Splash. The award-winning development involved the construction of a new wing (blue in the image) which houses a 100-bedroom hotel, with the rest of the building providing 45,000sq ft of retail space and over 300,000sq ft of office space. Sited next to the M6 motorway, the building makes a big impression on the thousands of people who pass by every day, especially at night when its large Fort Dunlop sign is illuminated.

Above: Birmingham Central Library.

The Birmingham Central Library was opened in 1974 and designed by John Madin, whose inverted concrete ziggurat architecture has been the focus of much debate. The library replaced the previous one opened in 1882, which itself replaced the first central library of 1865, which burnt down in 1879. One part of the previous buildings, the Shakespeare Memorial Room, has been preserved and incorporated into the new building. Plans are already afoot to replace the current building with a modern design by Dutch architects Mecanoo.

Opposite: The Chamberlain Memorial.

Erected in October 1880, the memorial commemorates Mayor Joseph Chamberlain, after whom Chamberlain Square was named. In recent years the memorial was restored and cleaned to reveal its pristine white Portland stone.

Left: Centenary Square.
Centenary Square was named in 1989 to commemorate the 100th anniversary of Birmingham becoming a city. There had been plans drawn up in the 1920s for a grand square, surrounded by civic buildings, to be built on top of the disused Gibsons Arm canal basin; however, only Baskerville House (in the top left of the photograph) and the Hall of Memory (centre) were built before construction was halted by the World War Two. There are now new plans for a library to be constructed on the car park next to Baskerville House.

Opposite: The Hyatt Regency Hotel.
The 75m-high Hyatt Regency Hotel, which contains 24 floors, was constructed in 1990 at a cost of £34 million as a joint venture between the city council and private enterprise. The hotel is attached directly to the International Conference Centre by the walkway in the bottom of the image.

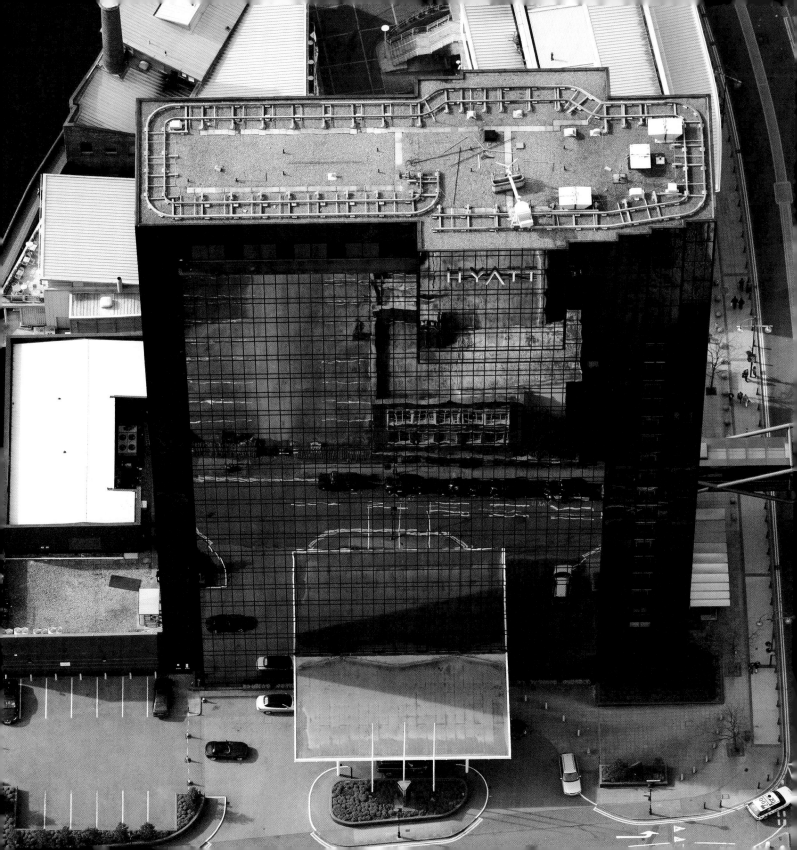

Above: Constitution Hill.
Built in 1896 for H.B. Sale, whose name it still carries, the terracotta building was designed by James Shaw and William Doubleday and is Grade II listed.

Opposite: The Spiral Café.
Designed by Marks Barfield Architects, the award-winning building's design was based on the theories of 13th-century mathematician Leonardo Fibonacci, who worked out the mathematics behind spiral forms.

Left: The new Queen Elizabeth Hospital. Photographed here as it neared completion in 2009, the new hospital is being constructed on the site of the existing Queen Elizabeth Hospital and will replace Selly Oak Hospital, concentrating most healthcare departments onto one super-site. Designed by BDP (Building Design Partnership) and constructed by Balfour Beatty, the £559 million project includes a 1,231-bed acute teaching hospital, A&E Dept and specialist burn and transplant wards.

Right: The British Telecom Tower.

Designed by M.H. Bristow and the Ministry of Public Works, the 500ft tower was constructed between 1963 and 1965, entering operational service in 1967. The fluted corners of the building are designed to improve airflow and aid stability, which is essential for the antennae to work properly. The structure has 26 floors plus five antennae decks on top and is surmounted by a crane used for raising equipment. BT is not the only occupant, as peregrine falcons are often seen on and around the structure.

Opposite: The Masshouse.

Part of the ongoing Eastside Development, the Masshouse building is constructed on the edge of what used to be the Masshouse Circus, part of the ring road built in the 1960s. The council is breaking this so-called 'Concrete Collar' and has removed the elevated sections of road so as to open up the way from the City centre to Eastside. The image shows Block One, a residential building, designed by Edward Cullinan Architects in conjunction with Aedas AHR. Constructed in 2007, it is the first part of the project to be completed and is noted for its distinctive cladding.

Opposite and above: Park Central.

This award-winning regeneration scheme is part-way through a 12-year build program which has transformed the 61-acre site into one of the most sought-after residential locations. When finished, there will be 1,700 new homes, 150,000sq ft of office space, a 250-bed hotel and eight acres of parkland. There are even plans for a combined heat and power community heating system to make this an environmentally-friendly project.

Left: Perrot's Folly.
When the tower was built in 1758 it stood in the middle of open parkland, but nowadays it stands in a residential area. From 1884 to 1979 the Grade II listed structure was used as a weather observatory. It has recently been restored and is occasionally open to the public for art exhibitions.

Opposite: The Victoria Law Courts.
Opened in 1891 by the Prince and Princess of Wales, the Grade I listed courts were designed by Sir Aston Webb and Ingress Bell. The courts are currently still in use as the local magistrates court, although there are plans to move them to a new building.

Right: Edgebaston Pumphouse.
Designed by J.H. Chamberlain and W. Martin, the pumphouse was constructed around 1870. It is thought that the chimney tower and nearby Perrot's Folly were the inspiration behind J.R.R. Tolkien's book *The Two Towers*, the second of the *Lord of the Rings* trilogy. Originally there was also a large engine house adjacent on the car park in the bottom right of the image, which was demolished. Fortunately, the rest of the building achieved a Grade II listing in 1979 so as to ensure its protection.

Right: The Rotunda:

Built in 1965, the 81m-high, Grade II listed Rotunda has recently been refurbished by Urban Splash and Glenn Howells Architects. Originally designed as offices by James A. Roberts, the building cost £1 million and was at first intended to have a revolving restaurant on the top floor, but this was cancelled at the last minute. Following the rebuilding, it now contains 234 apartments and has a new glass skin and atrium.

Left: The Birmingham Children's Hospital.

Birmingham is a cacophony of architectural styles, and almost all of them can be found together in one building with the Birmingham Children's Hospital, also known as the Diana, Princess of Wales, Hospital. Since its opening in 1862 it has changed and adapted to meet new challenges and needs. Even today, new facilities are being added, such as the new Paediatric Burns Centre and new Neonatal Surgery Unit, both part of a £19 million extension project. The Children's Hospital was moved to a new site built on Ladywood Road during World War One, and this site became the General Hospital until 1998 when the Children's Hospital was moved back to its original site. The paved area on the right of the image is occasionally used as a helicopter landing pad.

Above: The Town Hall.

Possibly Birmingham's most beautiful building the Grade I listed Town Hall was constructed between 1832 and 1834 to a design by J. A. Hansom and E. Welch which was inspired by the Roman Temple of Castor and Pollux. Shown here in pristine condition in 2008 just after it emerged from a £35 million restoration, the hall is used for meetings and concerts of all types, from Gospel to Rock and has hosted Charles Dickens, Edward Elgar, Felix Mendelssohn, The Beatles, Bob Dylan, The Proclaimers, Led Zeppelin and Margaret Thatcher.

Opposite: Victorian Shops.

Despite the 'Concretopolis' building programs of the 1960s and 1970s, Birmingham is full of little architectural gems, many surviving in obscure places. These two on Bristol Street (top) and Navigation Street (bottom) make a stark contrast to the modern steel shed retail parks of today.

Commerce

Right: The Bullring Shopping Centre.

There has been a market on this site since 1154, with the wool trade being of particular importance in the early Middle Ages and meat being a key trade later on. It is from the meat trade that the Bullring gets is name, a 'bull ring' being the iron ring where the bulls were tethered prior to slaughter.

Its not only commerce that has taken place at the Bullring, as it was also a popular place for political meetings in times gone by. Political tensions peaked on 1 July 1839 with the Bullring riots which took place when police attempted to break up a meeting of Chartists (Chartists were a group campaigning for electoral reform with a charter of demands such as universal male suffrage). This led to clashes between the Chartists and police, and eventually the army were called out.

The area was redeveloped in the 1960s, with the first Bullring Shopping Centre being opened in 1964. This first attempt was an unsuccessful 'Brutalise' concrete building, which was eventually demolished and replaced in 2003 with the current award-winning structures, designed by Benoy and Future Systems, who designed the 'Blobitecture'-style Selfridges store.

Previous page:
Sunday Market.

Above: The Bullring Bull.
The 6.5-ton bronze bull was designed by Laurence Broderick and is 4.5m from end to end.

Right: The Former Lucas Factory at Acocks Green.
Started as EIC Magnetos, the factory was bought by Lucas in 1925 and used to make dynamos and starter motors. At the end of World War Two they were making gas turbines, and through the 1950s and 1960s they made many of the automotive electrical parts to be found on a vast array of classic cars of the era. The factory was subsequently sold to Magneti Marelli and then to Denso, whose name it still carries. Shortly after this photograph was taken the factory was closed and is set to be demolished and replaced with a Florida-style retirement village. The adjacent Spring Road Station was opened in 1908 and is still in use, serving the Birmingham to Stratford line.

Opposite: The Jewellery Quarter, and above, in detail, the Chamberlain Clock.

Constructed in 1903 to commemorate Josef Chamberlain's visit to South Africa, the clock is sited in the heart of the Jewellery Quarter. Chamberlain was a local MP and Mayor who had lived on Frederick Street, which can be seen running from the centre to the top right of the image. The clock was rebuilt in the 1980s and now runs on a modern electric mechanism rather than the original clockwork one.

With more than 200 years of history, the Jewellery Quarter is still a centre for jewellery manufacture. Hundreds of jewellery workshops and retailers are still in the area, as well as other creative industries. At its peak just before World War One over 20,000 people were employed here and the area made a large proportion of the jewellery for the entire British Empire. Today it is a vibrant urban village whose conservation area status has preserved much of the Victorian industrial charm.

Right: The Mailbox.

One of the most striking buildings in Birmingham, the award-winning Mailbox sits surrounded by the modern architecture that signifies the city's resurgence. The building itself is not new, being converted by Associated Architects from a 1960s concrete mail sorting office. A new street has been cut through the centre of the building to connect through to the canal basin behind. The Mailbox now contains a shopping centre, hotel, offices, apartments and the studios for BBC Birmingham, which moved here when Pebble Mill was closed.

Above: GKN Aerospace Transparency Systems Factory at Kings Norton.
This was formerly the Triplex Safety glass plant, where glass has been manufactured since the 1930s, and today it manufactures aircraft, locomotive and bullet-resistant glass. In the foreground is the works football ground, home of Pilkington XXX FC. The Works League was very popular in the 20th century until the League finally folded at the end of the century. Formed as Triplex Safety Glass FC in 1931, the team still play in the Midland Combination Premier Division.

Right: Colmore Row.
Completed in 1976, the building was originally known as National Westminster House after its then owner. Designed by John Madin, the tower is 160m tall and has 23 stories. It has been empty since 2003, but in 2008 the new owners were given planning permission to demolish the structure and replace it with a new 35-story, 160m-tall tower designed by Hamilton Architects.

Above: Cadbury World.

In 1990 Cadbury opened up their factory to visitors to show how chocolate is made and to tell the story of the Cadbury family and Bournville. The attraction contains a replica of the original 1824 shop, the Cadbury-themed playground (above) and the world's biggest Cadbury shop.

Right: Cadbury Factory at Bournville.

Cadbury was started in 1824 when John Cadbury opened a shop selling drinks and chocolate. The business grew from there and before long he was manufacturing his own chocolate. When his sons George and Richard took over they opened the Bournville factory in 1879.

    The factory was more than just a place of production and, true to their Quaker beliefs, it was the centre of a model village including homes, schools and parks, planned by the brothers so their workers could live and work in a safe and healthy environment.

Right: Brindleyplace and the city centre.

Dominating the southern side of the city centre is the Brindleyplace development, which at 17 acres is the largest mixed-use development in the UK. The area had been an industrial site but by the 1970s it was in decline, and many buildings had become derelict. Starting in 1993, the scheme set about regenerating the area with an attractive canal-side development containing restaurants, shops, galleries, a theatre and the National Sea Life Centre. The first part of the scheme, 'The Water's Edge' retail centre, was completed in 1994. Since then, a number of buildings have been completed and work is still ongoing. The buildings have been designed by numerous different architects, helping to give each building its own individual style.

The Sea Life Centre is the grey building overlooking the canal junction in the image and contains a 6m-deep tank, traversed by a transparent tunnel through which visitors can gaze at a whole range of sea life, including sharks, stingrays and even otters.

Transport

Previous page: Spaghetti Junction. Officially known as the Gravelly Hill Interchange, this motoring wonder was opened in 1972 and connects the M6 to the A38M and a number of local roads. The site has long been used for transport infrastructure, with the railway, River Tame, Birmingham and Fazeley Canal, and the Tame Valley Canal all visible in the image.

Left: Farmer's Bridge flight of locks on the Birmingham and Fazeley Canal. The canal opened in 1789 to a design by John Smeaton and forms part of the Warwickshire ring of canals, connecting to the Coventry, Oxford, Grand Union and Stratford-upon-Avon Canals.

Opposite: Roundhouse Stable block, adjacent to the Birmingham Canal Navigations Junction with the Oozells Street Loop.

Above: The canals are now key to Birmingham's tourist industry, drawing thousands of visitors into the heart of the city every year. Guided canal cruises are a popular activity, and this one was photographed on the Icknield Port Loop. This loop is another left over by Telford's canal straightening and is currently rather run-down but is about to undergo a massive regeneration, similar to that already done around Brindley Place, to produce mixed leisure, commercial and tourism uses.

Opposite: Its well known that Birmingham has more miles of canal than Venice. This section, the Oozells Street Loop, was formed in 1829 when Thomas Telford reworked and straightened the original Birmingham Canal route James Brindley had built in 1769. The area has recently been redeveloped as an upmarket residential area.

Left: The Gas Street Basin.

Forming the junction of the Birmingham Canal Navigations Main Line and the Worcester and Birmingham Canal, the two canals were originally separated by the 'Worcester Bar' to prevent water flowing between them. The Worcester Bar is shown in the foreground with the brick footbridge ramp on it and partly obscured by buildings. This necessitated the transloading of all goods across the bar. Eventually this was rectified with the construction of the lock just visible adjacent to the brick footbridge ramp. Although the lock is still present, its gates are no longer used and have been removed. The footbridge is a modern reconstruction of those originally made by the Horseley Ironworks.

Opposite and above: The Tyseley Locomotive Works.
Opened in 1908 by the Great Western Railway, the loco works is now run by the Birmingham Railway Museum Trust and is used to service and restore vintage locomotives to Network Rail standards. Home to a number of locomotives in the Tyseley collection, the trust is dedicated to keeping vintage locomotives in use on mainline railways. Adjacent to the loco works are the modern railway sidings and London Midland Traincare Depot.

Above: Snow Hill Station.

Originally built by the Great Western Railway and opened in 1852 as Livery Street Station, it was renamed to Snow Hill Station in 1858. The station was rebuilt in 1871 with a glass and iron roof and then rebuilt again between 1906 and 1912.

In the 1960s Dr Beeching ordered the station's closure and the grand Edwardian buildings were demolished: the Great Western Hotel disappeared in 1969 and the station itself in 1977. Shortly after demolition, it was decided that a station on the site was a good idea after all, and a new station was constructed to a modern design by Seymour Harris Partnership, which opened in 1987. The station accommodates both mainline services and is the terminus for the Midland Metro line. The station is connected to Moor Street Station on the other side of the city centre by the Snow Hill Tunnel.

Left: Moor St Station.

This is an architectural gem; the only one of Birmingham's main stations to survive intact. The Grade II listed building was opened in 1908, with the permanent buildings completed in 1914. Originally intended as a terminus to relieve Snow Hill Station, it was threatened with closure by Dr Beeching, but as New Street Station had no spare capacity it remained in use for local services.

When Snow Hill Tunnel and Station were reopened, new platforms were built on the tunnel line on the right of the image with trains in. Currently these are the only platforms in use, although the original platforms are due to be put back in service very shortly. Until then they are occupied by a Great Western 0-8-0 steam locomotive, restored by the Tyseley Locomotive Works.

The station buildings have all been recently restored, and even the new platforms have been given a matching 1930s-style appearance. With help from the Birmingham Railway Museum Trust the station now includes preserved ironwork from the demolished Snow Hill Station.

Above: Birmingham New Street Station.
Originally opened in 1851, it had for a time the world's largest iron and glass roof, although this was eventually removed in the 1940s. During the 1960s the original station was replaced with the current structure, and this is now all set to be updated with a major redevelopment called 'Gateway Plus'.

Opposite: The remains of Curzon St Station.
Opened in 1838 as one of the world's first passenger stations, the Curzon Street Station was disadvantaged by being a little way out from the city centre. This led to it being replaced by New Street Station, although it continued in use as a goods station right up until 1966. The passenger entrance building by Philip Hardwick survives and is Grade 1 listed.

Above: New St Station signal box.

One of the most unusual buildings to receive listed building status is New Street Station's signal box, which was granted a Grade II listing in November 1995. Post-war buildings have to be of exceptional architectural quality to be listed. The five-storey signal box was constructed in 1964 in a Brutalist style, designed by Bicknall & Hamilton using wavy concrete panels hung on a concrete frame.

Opposite: Selly Oak Station.

Built for the Midland Railway and opened in 1876, the station was rebuilt in modern style in 1978. The original Victorian line was the single track in the top right of the image where a small section of the original bridge can still be seen. A large car park has been built, on what was once the goods sidings, and the station is an access point to the Park and Ride scheme.

On the left of the station is the Birmingham and Worcester Canal, constructed in 1795, which makes a very popular circular tourist route with the River Severn and the Staffordshire and Worcester Canal. There used to be a canal junction at the top of the photo with the Dudley No.2 Canal, but this closed after the Lapal Tunnel Collapsed.

Left: Five Ways.

At first glance Five Ways looks like a modern area without much of a history, but in actual fact it dates back to 1565, when it was first recorded. The area takes its name from the intersection of five roads. A sixth was added in 1820, but the name remained unchanged.

Just below the roundabout is the Birmingham Marriott Hotel, built in 1957 to a design by Cotton, Ballard & Blow, and just in front of it stands the recently restored memorial to Joseph Sturge, the anti-slavery campaigner.

On the left of the roundabout is the 68m high Metropolitan House, another John Madin-designed building, and then on the opposite side is the Five Ways Shopping Centre with Auchinleck House above it. Both constructed in 1964 and designed by Seymour Harris Architecture, they are about to receive a make over with new exterior cladding. In the future the roundabout may also have the Midland Metro Light Rail system running through it.

Previous page, left and opposite: The Birmingham St Patrick's Day Parade.

One of the biggest cultural events in Birmingham is the annual St Patrick's Day parade, which is the largest outside Dublin and New York. The whole city is turned into a moving mass of emerald green, with floats, music, dancing and marching bands.

Above and opposite: Birmingham Cathedral.

Dedicated to St Phillip, the baroque cathedral was opened as a parish church in 1715. Designed by Thomas Archer, with extensions by J.A. Chatwin, the church became a cathedral, England's third-smallest, when the Diocese of Birmingham was created in 1905. Although badly damaged in the war, fortunately many key items, including its stained glass windows, were removed to a place of safety at the beginning of the war allowing it to be fully restored in 1948. St Phillip's still has its original organ, albeit in modernised form, and in 1952 the cathedral received a Grade I listing.

Above: Catacombs at Warstone Cemetery.

Opened in 1847 and designed by J.R. Hamilton, the cemetery is closed to new burials but is a popular place for a peaceful stroll, with the headstones telling their own stories of Birmingham's past. While modern cemeteries tend to be laid out in basic easy-to-maintain plots, Victorian cemeteries were laid out as grand parks to remember the deceased. The park is Grade II on the National Register of Historic Parks and Gardens.

The catacombs themselves had a surprising role in World War Two, as they were used by people to shelter from the bombing, an eerie place to spend the night!

Above: The Birmingham Central Mosque.
Opened in 1975, the mosque is the second oldest and one of the largest purpose-built mosques in the United Kingdom. Friday prayers are attended by up to 5,000 people, and during the festival of Eid up to 20,000 people will visit the mosque.

Left: The Dhamma-Talaka Peace Pagoda.
Opened in 1998, the Birmingham Buddhist Vihara Pagoda is built in the form of an oriental sacred tower, modelled on the Shwedagon Pagoda in Burma.

Opposite: St Paul's Church.
Opened in 1779, the Grade I listed building was designed by Wolverhampton-based architect Roger Eykyn, with the spire being added in 1823. The surrounding square which takes its name from the church has had some ups and downs over the years. Originally it was a well-to-do residential area, but much was changed into commercial use as the Jewellery Quarter expanded. With the decline in the 20th century, the area became quite run-down but is now enjoying a renaissance, with most of the surviving buildings restored and listed.

Above: Gurdwara Babe Ke.
The new Sikh Temple, Gurdwara Babe Ke, at Soho Hill, Hockley, shown in the final stages of construction. Gurdwara translates from the Punjabi as 'doorway to the guru'.

Opposite: St Martin's Church.
The Grade II listed church was constructed in 1873 to a design by J.A. Chatwin and replaced earlier churches which trace their history on this site back to 1290. The tower remains from the previous church and contains an unusually large peal of 16 bells.

Above: The Peace Gardens.
Originally St Thomas's Church, which was destroyed by bombing in 1940, the gardens were landscaped in 1995 to commemorate the 50th anniversary of the war's end. In 1998, during the nearby G8 conference, a number of world leaders planted commemorative trees in the garden.

Opposite: The Wheel of Birmingham.
An occasional visitor to Birmingham, this 60m-high Ferris wheel was first seen in Paris for the Millennium celebrations. A number of these wheels have been made by Ronald Bussink in the Netherlands, and the structure is portable, being supported by water ballast in tanks at the base.

Above: Frankfurt Christmas Market.
Birmingham's Frankfurter 'Weihnachtsmarkt' is the largest German Christmas market outside Germany or Austria and attracts more than 2 million visitors a year. The market celebrates the important relationship with Birmingham's twin city Frankfurt am Maine. With over 640 British businesses in Frankfurt and large numbers of German businesses in Birmingham, the bilateral trade is of immense importance to both cities' economies.

Opposite: Singers Hill Synagogue.
The Birmingham Hebrew Congregation Synagogue was built in 1856 to a design by Yeoville Thomason. There has been a Jewish community in Birmingham since the 18th century, and this synagogue was built to replace previous buildings in Severn Street and Hurst Street.

Above and opposite: The Custard Factory.

Originally the factory where Bird's Custard was manufactured, the site has now been transformed into a vibrant media and arts centre.

The story started in 1837 when Sir Alfred Bird cooked up a cornflower-based sauce because his wife was allergic to eggs. His recipe proved a hit, and the nation went custard potty, so much so that in its heyday the factory employed up to 1,000 people. The product is still made, but production moved away from here in the early 1980s.

The buildings were restored and redeveloped, starting in 1992, with the work overseen by local architects Glenn Howells. The first phase created over 300 jobs in arts and media related positions, and it is hoped the location will again see 1,000 jobs when it is finished. As well as hundreds of studios, there are shops, galleries, dance studios, a theatre, a café and a restaurant. The work is still ongoing, as can be seen by the hoardings on Devonshire House on the right, with future proposals including an exhibition centre and a riverside walk and a new bridge over the River Rea.

Right: Birmingham's Chinese Quarter.

Birmingham's Chinese Quarter first started to emerge as a cluster of Chinese businesses in the 1960s and has since grown into the vibrant community we see today. The heart of the community is the Arcadian Centre in the foreground, with numerous shops and restaurants around a circular piazza. The area really comes alive for the Chinese New Year celebrations.

Also in the image on the left side is the Birmingham Hippodrome Theatre, opened in 1899, which is home of the Birmingham Royal Ballet. The building has been remodeled several times over the last hundred years, with the new façade in the image being constructed in 2000.

The area has not lost touch with its history, and in the bottom left corner you can see Birmingham's last surviving back-to-back houses, which are now preserved as a museum.

Education

Above and opposite: Aston University.
Founded as the School of Metallurgy in 1875, the university received its charter in 1966. The Gosta Green site was acquired in 1933, and the main building was constructed in 1951 to a design by Ashley & Newman. Today the university has 1,250 staff members and 9,000 students, who voted it 11th-best in the National Union of Students survey. Research areas include vision sciences, photonics, neuroimaging energy and sustainability, with some big successes to its credit such as the development of the brain cancer drug Temozolomide.

Previous page: University of Birmingham.
Founded in 1900, the University of Birmingham was the first red-brick university and also the first to establish a medical school. The main Edgebaston campus is based around its original Edwardian architecture, designed by Aston Webb and Ingress Bell, with the Joseph Chamberlain Clock Tower, the largest free-standing clock tower in the world, in the centre. Today the university is involved in pioneering work in cancer research and nanotechnology.

Above: Millennium Point.
Millenium Point is a mixed-use development containing a number of businesses and organisations. It is also home to the Technology Innovation Centre and the Birmingham School of Acting, both run by the Birmingham City University. Currently the university has a number of campuses spread around the city and is planning to move many to a new £150 million campus at the Eastside development nearby.

Above: Birmingham City University North Campus.

Originally the Birmingham Polytechnic, it was created from the merger of five colleges in 1972 and became a university in 1992. A wide range of subjects are taught in the Northern Campus, including Marketing, Finance, Computing, History and English. Facilities include broadcast and drama studios and a mock law court.

Behind the University is the Perry Bar Stadium. Built as an athletics stadium, it is now used for Greyhound Racing and Speedway racing.

Left: Birmingham City University Edgbaston Campus.

Home to healthcare students, courses taught here include Nursing, Midwifery and related healthcare courses. The campus is home to the Royal Centre for Defence Medicine and has recently undergone a £30 million redevelopment. New facilities include a virtual operating suite which allows medical students to practice surgery on virtual patients.

Also in the image are the Birmingham Botanical Gardens, on the left, which were designed by J.C. Louden and opened in 1832. In the centre foreground is St George's Church by J.J. Scholes, opened in 1838. J.R.R. Tolkien lived at a couple of the houses in the image.

Above: The Handsworth Technical College.
Opened in 1881 as the Handsworth Methodist College, it was designed by Messrs Goddard and Ball in exuberant High Victorian style with castellated tower and much use of terracotta. The hall within the semicircular garden was the original college chapel. Today the site is used as university halls of residence and is Grade II listed.

Above: Moseley School.
Constructed in 1857, the school's main building was designed by Joseph James. During World War One it was used as a military barracks. Today it is a comprehensive school and language college, teaching French, German, Urdu, Chinese and Spanish, with courses at GCSE and A level available, as well as adult education classes. The school provides exchange visits for pupils and works with partner schools in Germany, Pakistan and South Africa. The school also provides Urdu courses for public services and NHS staff.

Right: The Newman University College.
Founded in 1968, the Newman University College was originally a teacher training college but now provides a wider range of courses, including undergraduate foundation and postgraduate degrees, as well as a number of short courses. The university college has been ranked as the best in the country and was also top for student satisfaction in the 2009 Guardian University League tables.

Above: Edward VI Handsworth School.
Founded in 1883, the school is a voluntary aided grammar school for girls. Ofsted has recently rated the school as outstanding for the fourth time. The school gained performing arts specialist status in 2003. In 2007 every pupil gained five A* to C GCSEs, including English and Mathematics, with the majority of students gaining A or A* grades.

Opposite: King Edward V/Five Ways School.
Founded in 1883, the school is now the West Midlands's largest co-educational state grammar school. The Five Ways in the name refers to its original location, with the school moving to its current site at Bartley Green in 1958. Since 2004 the school has been a Humanities Specialist School, the first in Birmingham, and since 2008 also has science as a secondary specialism. Ofsted has also rated this school as outstanding four years in a row, with a Grade 1 in all 38 categories.

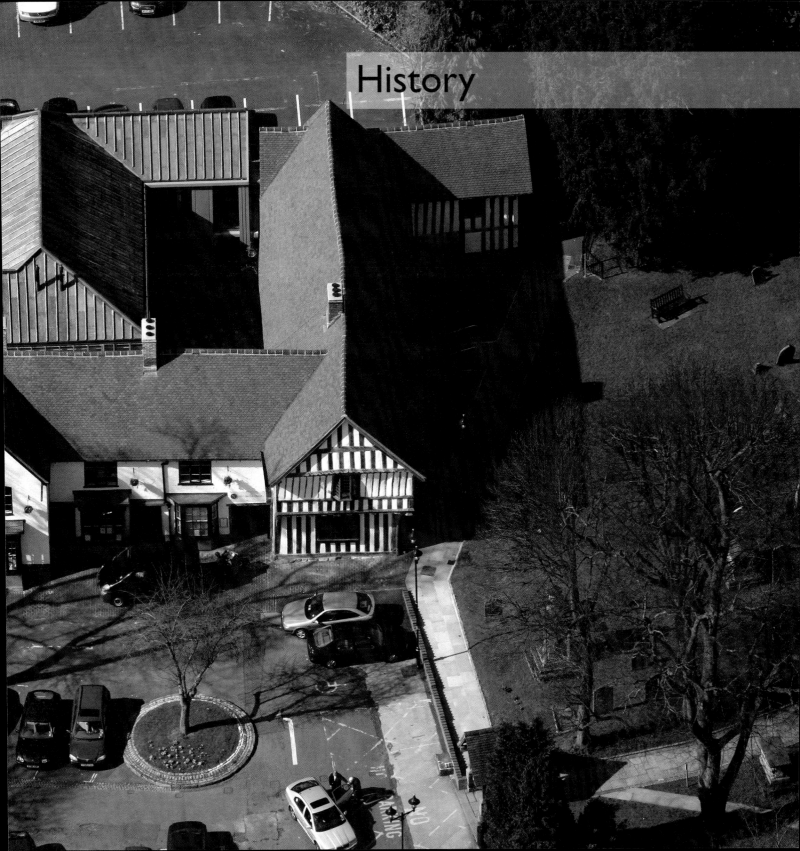

Above: The Birmingham Gun Barrel Proof House.

Early black-powder guns were prone to explode, so in 1813 the Proof House was built to test-fire guns before sale, a practice which became mandatory in 1868. The Grade II listed building is still used for its original purpose and also contains a small museum.

Previous page: The Saracens Head at Kings Norton.

Built in 1492 by Humphrey Rotsey, who was a Tudor merchant, the house was extended in the 16th century, and in July 1643 Queen Henrietta Maria stayed here while amassing troops to reinforce her husband, Charles I, in York. From 1771 until 1930 it was used as an inn. Together with the Old Grammar School and St Nicholas Church, the three buildings are known as Saint Nicholas Place and are open to the public.

Opposite Page: Edgbaston Hall.

Originally a mediaeval manor house, Edgbaston Hall was made into a stronghold during the Civil War by Colonel 'Tinker' Fox who used it as a base to raid nearby Royalist areas. The Manor was badly damaged and then burnt down altogether by Puritans in 1688. The current building was built in 1717 to a design by Richard Gough, with gardens by Capability Brown.

Left: Selly Manor.

The oldest parts of Selly Manor date from the early 14th century, with a number of Tudor additions. By the end of the 19th century it was in poor condition and being used as tenements. In 1907 there were proposals put forward to demolish it, but fortunately the house was rescued by George Cadbury, who dismantled it and moved it to its current location at Bournville. The painstaking work took four years, but by 1917 it was again complete.

Behind the manor is the 13th-century Minworth Greaves Medieval Hall, which was also rescued by George Cadbury. Both buildings are open to the public and also contain the Laurence Cadbury collection of furniture.

Above: The Birmingham Mint.
Built in 1862 for Ralph Heaton & Sons, the mint manufactured coins for private and government customers worldwide. When completed, it was the largest private mint in the world, with customers including the governments of France, Italy, Russia and the UK. Although the mint was busy right up to the introduction of the Euro, there was also a loss of business with the Royal Mint, and in 2003 the Birmingham Mint was sold, with much of the machinery being shipped off to India. The site is being redeveloped with new buildings incorporating the Grade II listed façade.

Opposite: The George Cadbury Memorial Carillon.
Bournville Junior School has an unusual addition in the form of a 48-bell carillon. Built by George Cadbury in 1906, with the original bells made by John Taylor & Co, it is said Cadbury was inspired by the bells of Bruges Town Hall. The carillon is still played every Saturday. A carillon of bells is not rung in the way church bells are rung but is instead played by a carillonneur like an organ. The adjacent infants' school was completed in 1910.

Above: Site of the Soho Manufactory.

Built in 1766 by Mathew Boulton and John Fothergill, the Soho Manufactory was one of the world's first mass production centres and claimed, at the time, to be the largest in the world. Adjacent was the Soho Mint, which would have been on the left of this image, and on the right the large white house is Boulton's home, Soho House, which is still standing 200 years after Boulton's death. Today the Grade II listed house is a museum dedicated to Boulton and his associates in the Lunar Society, the leading scientific group of its day.

The manufactory made a vast array of products such as clocks, buttons, buckles, tableware and silverware, many using early assembly line techniques. Some of the first practical factory steam engines were developed here by James Watt. The manufactory was demolished in 1868 to allow the construction of the houses you see in the photograph, however, underneath the gardens; still lie the foundations of the manufactory, something which was re-discovered in the *Time Team* television program.

Above: St Nicholas Church.

The Grade I listed church of St Nicholas is so old nobody knows exactly how old it is. It was certainly here in the 12th century, but it may also have been a Saxon chapel. The church was enlarged in the 13th century and rebuilt in the 14th. The spire was added in the 15th century, and significant renovations and alterations were carried out in the 17th and 19th centuries. From 1940 to 1946 the curate was the Revd W. Awdry who wrote the *Thomas the Tank Engine* books. He wrote the first book in 1943 for his young son, which reached a wider audience when they began to be published in 1946. On the right of the image is the Old Grammar School which featured in the BBC's *Restoration* television program.

Left: Weoley Castle.

Following the conquest of England by William Duke of Normandy in 1066, the area that is now Weoley Castle was given to a Norman, William Fitz Ansculf, who was made Baron of Dudley. He built a fortified manor house consisting of little more than a few wattle and daub buildings surrounded by palisade and moat.

In late 1264 Rodger de Somery was granted a licence to crenellate by Henry III, and the site was reconstructed in stone. Following his death, this work was completed by his sister and her husband, John and Joan Botetourts, finishing the construction with a hall, chapel, gatehouse and curtain wall with towers. After their deaths the castle was inherited by the Berkley family, but in 1485 Sir Thomas Berkley found himself on the losing side at Bosworth Field. After Richard III was defeated the victorious Henry Tudor confiscated the castle and estates.

The estate was later bought by a merchant called Richard Jervoise, who rented out the lands but allowed the castle to fall into ruin. His descendants owned the castle until 1809 when it was sold to Daniel Ledsam. Following the death of his descendent James Coddington in 1929, the estate was sold to the City of Birmingham, who built the housing estate on it.

Above and opposite: Metchley Roman Fort.

This was the site of one of the Romans' major forts, which in its earlier and larger phase measured some 200m². The original fort was defended by a double ditch and covered the area from the hospital entrance car park just above the roundabout to the tiled roof building in the foreground and across to just above the chimney on the left. The tree line running top to bottom marks the western edge of the fort. Outside the main fort was a vicus (civilian settlement) to the west/left under the red tile-roofed building, plus defended annexes on each of the other sides which lay under the main hospital building and under the area on the left and bottom of the image.

The original and larger version of the fort was constructed only a few years after the Romans' successful invasion of Britain in AD 43 and was probably built as part of the process of conquering and subduing the native Britons, some of whom were expressing reservations about being Romanised. It is likely that troops from here would have taken part in the defeat of Boudica in the Battle of Watling Street around AD 60.

Once resistance was crushed, the fort was remodelled into a smaller version to house a smaller garrison. Remains of the fort were visible on the ground until the hospital was built in 1938 and have been extensively excavated. The north-west corner ditch has been reconstructed and the location of the corner tower marked with wooden posts (above).

Above and opposite: Edgbaston Reservoir.
Following the recent Olympic games, Britain is the world's leading rowing nation, and throughout the land rowers can be found training on all suitable stretches of water. Edgbaston Reservoir is no exception, being shared between Birmingham Schools Rowing Association, Birmingham University and Birmingham Rowing Club. Opposite we can see a women's eight out on a training run.

Previous page: Birmingham City Football Club.
Opened in 1906, Birmingham's St Andrew's ground seats 30,000 fans; although, in the past before it became an all-seated stadium it could hold crowds of over 65,000. Founded in 1875 as the Small Heath Alliance, the club was promoted into the Premier League at the end of the 2008–09 season.

Right: Aston Villa Football Club's Villa Park Stadium.

Built in 1897, Villa Park currently has capacity for 42,000 fans, making it the eighth largest in the country. Founded in 1874, Aston Villa play in the Premier League and are great rivals of Birmingham City, against whom they play the 'Second City Derby'.

Above: Kart Track.
One of the newer sports to enthral the younger generation is Karting. Many of the world's top racing drivers have started their careers in karting. The Grand Prix Karting circuit is just under a kilometre in length, which allows the fastest 270cc Thunderkarts to reach speeds of 70 mph.

Opposite: Weoley Hill Cricket Club.
One of a number of grass roots cricket clubs in Birmingham, Weoley Hill Cricket Club is a member of the Warwickshire Cricket League.

Above: The Alexander Stadium.
Opened in 1975, the Alexander Stadium is Birmingham's premier athletics venue and has staged the Amateur Athletics Association Championships and the Disability World Athletics Championships. Situated in Perry Park, Perry Bar, the stadium recently had the new High Performance Centre added, which is visible in the top-right of the image..

Previous page: Edgbaston Cricket Ground.
Home to Warwickshire County Cricket Club, the 21,000-seater ground was first used in 1886. There are now plans for a £30 million modernisation of the ground, which will include new seating, media facilities, a museum and hotel.

Opposite: American Football.
American football is growing in popularity in the UK, and Birmingham has a number of teams. Here the Bristol Aztecs Youth team meet the Lancashire Wolverine Colts on the Birmingham University playing fields in front of the Queen Elizabeth Hosiptal.

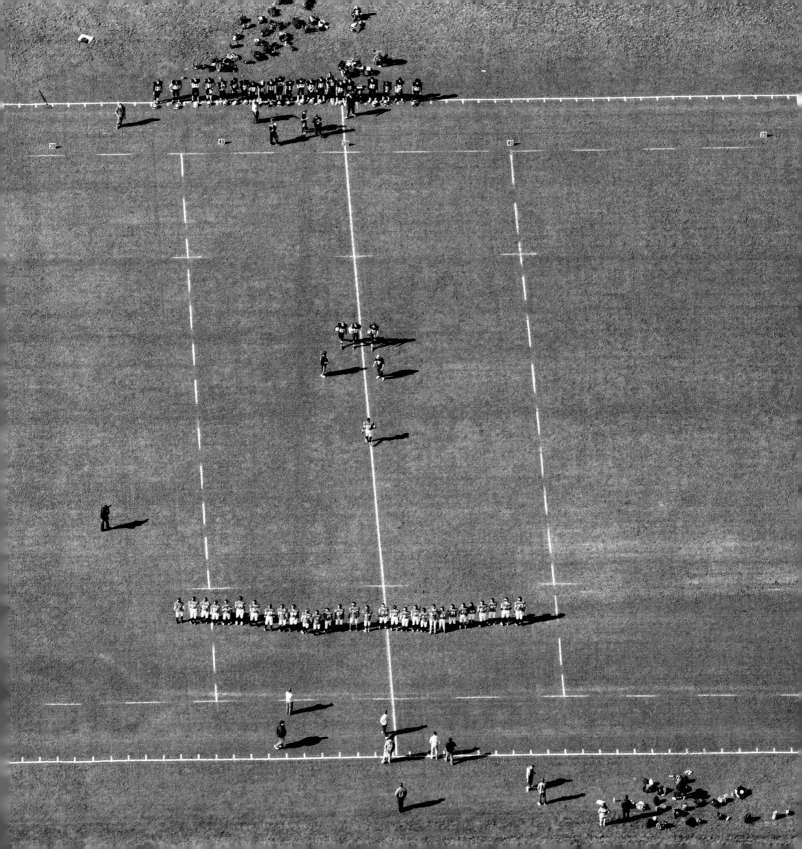

Above: The National Indoor Arena.

When it opened in 1991 the NIA was the largest indoor arena in the country, with an area of 10,000 square metres and a capacity of up to 13,000 visitors. The building is constructed right over the top of the main Birmingham to London railway line. The arena is used to host conferences, exhibitions, concerts and a wide range of sporting events, including trampoline, badminton, indoor rowing, wrestling and the 2009 Judo World Cup. The *Gladiators* television program was also filmed here.

Opposite: Football.

Another football match at Birmingham University's Metchley Lane playing fields – this time it is the more common English soccer.

135

Above and opposite: Kings Norton Skate Park.
Situated in Kings Norton Park, the new skate park is one of very few which is completely free, providing a vital energy outlet for youngsters with skateboards and BMX bikes.

Above: Hall Green Greyhound Track.
Opened on 4 August 1927, Hall Green was Birmingham's first greyhound track, being built only a year after the sport arrived in the country. The track is 412m long, and a greyhound can do 480m in around 28 seconds, which is twice as fast as a human. The stadium also contains a hotel and a snooker club. Although greyhound racing is past its peak (the height of the sport's popularity was reached in the 1940s), there are still 28 stadiums dotted around the UK.

Opposite: Weoley Hill Tennis Club and Bowling Club.
The recently renovated porous tarmacadam courts of Weoley Hill Tennis Club make a colourful sight from above. Affiliated to the Warwickshire Lawn Tennis Association, the club has an active membership of both adults and juniors, with coaching provided.

Next to the tennis club is the Weoley Hill Bowling Club, which has been going since 1928 when it was opened by George Cadbury.

Suburbs

Above: Acock's Green.
The aptly named Circular Road sits in Acock's Green, right in the heart of Birmingham's leafy suburbs. Acock's Green is named after the Acock family who lived here in 1370.

Previous page: Longbridge.
Longbridge is dominated by the motor works. Formerly Austin, then British Leyland, it finished its days as MG Rover, which went into receivership in 2005. Although volume car manufacturing is gone, out of the ashes has arisen the MG motor company who is again manufacturing new versions of the MG TF sports car. The older parts of the car plant, not used for the new TF, have been demolished, and plans are in place to redevelop these in what will be Birmingham's largest regeneration project, which will see the construction of 1,450 new homes and the creation of up to 10,000 jobs. There will be a learning quarter, new shopping centre, urban park and an Austin museum to remember the cars once built here.

Opposite: Rubery.
Rubery is dominated by the former motor works in neighbouring Longbridge, which provided work for many of Rubery's residents. Recently the new Great Park scheme in the centre right of the image has regenerated the area with new shops, leisure facilities and a multiplex cinema.

Opposite and above: Sparkhill

Lying to the south east of Birmingham City centre is the suburb of Sparkhill, which takes its name from the the nearby Spark Brook. The area was farmed in the middle ages, and Roman coins have been found in the vicinity, indicating much earlier activity.

Sparkhill's two best-known buildings are the Art Deco swimming pool, opened in 1931 (with the chimney above), and the library (with the clock tower above) by Arthur Harrison, which was built between 1898 and 1902. Originally it was the Council House for the then Yardley District Council but was turned into a library in 1923. Next to it stand the fire station, police station and court which houses the West Midlands Police Museum.

Opposite: 19th-century terraced housing in Sparkhill

Right: Harborne

In modern times Harborne is an upmarket residential area with its High Street, right, crammed with upmarket shops and restaurants, a far cry from its origins as an agricultural village surrounded by farmland. The village was mentioned in the *Doomsday Book* and remained relatively small until the arrival of the Harborne Railway in 1874, which caused a rapid expansion to cater for the new middle-class commuters.

Above: Site of the Harborne Railway.

Now long gone, the Harborne Railway used to run from the railway bridge, in the top left of the image, to the station, turntable and sidings where the flat-roofed apartment buildings are now. There had been proposals for the line to link to Halesowen and Bromsgrove Railway, but in the end only the two miles to the LNWR line near the city centre were ever built. The passenger service succumbed to faster and more frequent bus competition in the 1930s, and the good service remained until the 1950s, servicing the adjacent Chad Valley Toy Factory. The last train ever was an enthusiasts' special in 1963.

Opposite: Moorpool.

One of Britain's first purpose-built Garden Suburbs, the Moorpool estate was built around the pool, with particular attention to providing a green and pleasant environment with lots of gardens and open spaces such as allotments. Recent proposals to add some modern housing to the estate have not been universally welcome. With so many green, open spaces, the area is rich in wildlife including frogs, newts, toads, pipistrelle bats, dragonflies, water voles and 47 species of birds, including tawny owls and some species under threat such as the lesser-spotted woodpecker.

Above: Lozells.

Running across the centre of the image is a very straight road, Wheeler Street. The reason it is so straight is because the Romans built it, and it would have originally led to the Metchley Roman fort where Birmingham University is now. On Wheeler Street. are the Holte Visual and Performing Arts College and the adjacent Lozells junior, infants' and nursery schools. These are all set to be demolished and replaced with modern buildings as part of the £140 milllion Building Schools for the Future programme.

Opposite: Selly Oak.

Shot in Autumn, this view shows the beautiful Autumn colours of the trees around Castle Road and Bushwood Road. Until modern times the whole area was largely wooded with a few clearings for settlement. The area was mentioned in the *Doomsday Book* of 1085, when it was referred to as 'Escelie'.

Above: Houses on Harborne Lane.

Previous page: Looking north across Edgbaston.
For a city, Birmingham is a very green environment, as this view clearly shows. The area has always been covered in woodlands, right back to when the Romans built their fort which would have been in the centre right of this image. The wide open fairways of the Edgbaston Golf Club can be seen above the university on the right, and in the top left is Edgbaston Reservoir. Running up the right side of the image, on its way to the city centre, is the Worcester and Birmingham canal, opened in 1815.

Opposite: Edgbaston.
At the northern end of Edgbaston, near the reservoir, we have Hagley Road and just above it the Grade II listed St Augustine's Church with the 185ft spire towering high above the surrounding suburbia. Built in 1868, St Augustine's was designed by Julius A.Chatwin, who also designed St Martin's at the Bullring. The area around the church is a conservation area, hopefully ensuring this suburban view will not change radically in the future.

Left: Stirchley.
The double ellipse of Birch Road and Greenoak Crescent make a striking sight when viewed from above. In the middle is the octagonal Church of the Ascension, which was built to replace the original church, which burnt down in 1965. The new church, designed by Romilly Craze, opened on 14 July 1973 at a cost of £70,000 and features a fibre glass statue of Christ over its main entrance.

Above: Bartely Green.
First mentioned in the *Doomsday Book* of 1086, when it was referred to as Berchlai, Bartley Green has probably been settled since Saxon times; indeed, the name is derived from Saxon / Old English meaning a clearing among Birch trees. In modern times the area is now a large housing estate, with little to remind us of the Saxon farmers who once ploughed here with their ox teams.

Opposite: St Agnes Church Wake Green.
Constructed between 1883 and 1893, the church was designed by William Davies. The tower was added in 1932 to a design by C.E. Bateman. The church is Grade II listed as are a number of the nearby houses, many of which reflect the Arts and Crafts movement of the time. The area around the church was designated a conservation area in 1987. In the centre left of the image, the second house rear to the camera was the home of Fredrick W. Lanchester, founder of the Lanchester Motor Company.

Right: Wake Green.

This wide view looks out over Wake Green, Moseley and Sparkhill in the direction of the City Centre. A careful eye will reveal the Edgbaston Cricket ground in the centre background, Birmingham University on the left edge and St Agnes's Church in the centre foreground. The pond in the centre foreground was originally a mill pond for 'Lady Mill', which was in use from the 15th to 19th centuries. The playing fields on the lower right of the image are believed to have contained an earthwork indicative of Iron or Bronze age habitation. Unfortunately the area was ploughed, and currently nothing is visible. The wooded area on the lower edge of the playing field contained a windmill, which was known to have existed there in the mid-17th century.

Above: Bournville Boating Lake.

When George Cadbury planned the model village of Bournville he was sure to include lots of green recreation space for his workers. The green space included parkland, and the Boating Lake at Valley Parkway opened in 1932. The lake was all hand-built by unemployed workers and is still in use today. It is home to the Bournville Model Yacht & Power Boats Club for whom it was created. The 85-year-old club is one of the oldest in the country.

Above: Highgate.

Highgate was probably the location of the original Anglo-Saxon settlement that evolved into Birmingham, with people living along the banks of the River Rea in the top left of the image. The name comes from Old English/ Saxon meaning the home of Berms followers or descendants. Birmingham was mentioned in the *Doomsday Book,* but the name Highgate does not appear until the 18th century, by which time it had evolved into an upmarket residential area which contained a large mansion called Highgate House. Further large houses were built in the early 19th century, some of which can still be seen on New Moseley Road on the right edge of the image. Towards the end of the 19th and early 20th century large numbers of terraced houses were built; however, many of these were destroyed when the area was heavily bombed in World War Two.

Buildings of interest include St Albans church, built in 1881 on Conybere St in the centre left of the image, and Rowton House, now the Paragon Hotel, in the top right, with the copper spires, built in 1903.

Above: Kings Heath.

For most of recorded history Kings Heath was relatively sparsely populated heathland. Things began to change when the road was upgraded to a turnpike road in 1767, and the Heath was enclosed in 1772. Further development occurred when the railway arrived in 1840, allowing wealthy business owners to live here and commute to the city. The station is now gone but was by the bridge on the left of the photograph. Also long gone are the trams, which used to trundle up and down the High Street from 1887 until 1949.

Opposite: All Saints Church, Kings Heath.

Constructed in 1860 to a design by F. Preedy, the spire was added in 1866, and extensions by J.A. Chatwin were added at the end of the century. The area in the top left of the image used to be the Tram Depot and marked the end of the tram-line from Birmingham. Onward travel passengers would take a horse-drawn cab from the cab station, which was in the lower right corner of the image.

Overleaf: Waterloo Road, Kings Heath.

On the left is Grange Road, which takes its name from a large 18th-century house called The Grange which stood here until it was demolished in the 1890s to allow the construction of these houses that stand in what was the garden. Grange Road itself was the driveway to the Grange. In July 2005 the area was hit by a freak tornado, with wind speeds of up to 130mph, which ripped off many roofs and caused widespread damage throughout the Kings Heath and surrounding areas.